KETO DIET COOKBOOK

(A BEGINNER'S GUIDE):

Top New Healthy and Delicious Ketogenic Recipes:
A Proven and Most Effective Guide to Achieve Your Weight Loss Goal
and Shred Fat Fast.

By

DAVIS POWELL

Copyright © 2019, By: DAVIS POWELL

ISBN-13: 978-1-950772-14-8
ISBN-10: 1-950772-14-4

All Rights Reserved. No part of this publication may be reproduced in any form or by any means, including scanning, photocopying, or otherwise without prior written permission of the copyright holder.

Disclaimer:

The information provided in this book is designed to provide helpful information on the subjects discussed. The publisher and author are not responsible for any specific health or allergy needs that may require medical supervision and are not liable for any damages or negative consequences from any treatment, action, application or preparation, to any person reading or following the information in this book.

Table of Contents

- Lose Weight by Achieving Optimal Ketosis 5
- TIPS TO GET YOU STARTED ON THE KITOGENIC DIET 6
- Mustard Balsamic Baked Chicken Recipe 7
- Skillet Rosemary Chicken Recipe 9
- Coconut-Buttermilk Southwestern Grilled 11
- Slow Cooker Chipotle Barbacoa Brisket 13
- Rosemary Ranch Chicken Kabobs Recipe 15
- Chicken and Pineapple Skewers Recipe 17
- Chicken Drumsticks with Orange Glaze 19
- Sweet Garlic Chicken Recipe 21
- Slow Cooker Buffalo Chicken Meatballs 23
- Slow Cooker Queso Chicken Chili Recipe 25
- Meat loaf with mushrooms recipe 27
- Beanless chili recipe 29
- Hearty beef stew recipe 31
- Roast beef with thyme, garlic and red wine 33
- Bacon-wrapped mini meatloaves Recipe 35
- Sirloin Steak with Avocado Salad Recipe 37
- Grilled Steak and Summer Veggies Recipe 39
- Veal Chops with Rosemary Recipe 41
- Beef Brisket with Fall Vegetables Recipe 43
- Salmon tartare with fresh herbs recipe 45
- Tuna Burger Recipe 47
- Salmon Florentine Recipe 49
- Grilled Shrimp Skewers with Watermelon and Avocado Recipe 51
- Shrimp Burgers with Pineapple-Avocado 53
- Bacon-Wrapped Salmon Recipe 55
- Bigos Recipe 57
- Thai Pork Lettuce Wraps Recipe 59
- Pork Chop with Peaches Recipe 61
- Homemade Ham Recipe 63
- Spicy Spare Ribs Recipe 65
- Pork and Apple Meatloaf Recipe 67
- Chicken with Mushroom Cream Sauce 69
- Chicken and Artichoke Panzanella Recipe 71
- Grilled Chicken and Pineapple with Onion Relish Recipe 73
- Sun-dried Tomato Chicken Recipe 75
- Thai Larb Recipe 76
- Zaatar Grilled Chicken Recipe 78
- Spicy drumstick recipe 80

Grilled Pork with Basil Rub Recipe 81
Spicy Pork Chili Recipe 82
Pork Tenderloin with Burgundy Sauce Recipe 84
Crab Stuffed Shrimp Recipe 86
Smoked Salmon Salad in Cucumber Slices 88
Pomegranate Salmon Recipe 89
Grilled Maple Dijon Salmon with Bacon 91
Lomi Lomi Salmon 93
Tuna with Avocado Salsa 94
Scallop Tartare with Strawberries Recipe 96
Grilled Salmon-Tomato Skewers Recipe 97
Oysters Kilpatrick Recipe 99
Roasted asparagus 101
Cuban Shredded Beef Recipe 102
Barbecued Sirloin in Dijon Recipe 104
Simple Summer Chicken Recipe 105
Grilled Chicken with Lime Butter Recipe 106
Kansas City BBQ Wings Recipe 108
BBQ Chicken and Bacon Bites Recipe 110
Chicken with Lime and Avocado Salad Recipe 111
Turkey Chili Recipe 113
Slow Cooked Bacon-Wrapped Chicken Recipe 115
Spicy Sriracha Chicken Wings Recipe 116
Honey-mustard Drumsticks Recipe 118
Conclusion 119

INTRODUCTION

Lose Weight by Achieving Optimal Ketosis

When your diet is carbs deficiency, the level of glycogen in your body drops and you enter ketosis (which is a process in which your brain burns ketone bodies using energy from your fat to avoid draining the protein stores in your muscles)

The major aim of a low carb, ketogenic diet plan is to attain a metabolic state called ketosis. Ketosis helps the body survive during times when no food is available. Research has shown it to improve disease conditions such as epilepsy, autism, cancer, Alzheimer's and others.

A ketogenic diet plan requires tracking the amount of carb intake in your daily meal and keeping carbohydrate intake between 20-60 grams each day. The daily protein requirement should be moderate and it all depends on height, gender and how much exercise one does each day. In addition, the balance of calories will be from fats. These ratios ensure that you go into ketosis and stay there, which is the main aim of the ketogenic diet.

However, the nutrient intake on a ketogenic diet typically works out to 20-25% from protein, 5-10% from carbohydrate and about 70-75% of calories from fat on a daily basis when calories are not restricted.
Finally, the major benefit of ketosis is that it increases the body's ability to utilize fats for fuel and it also has a protein-sparing effect.

Additionally, another benefit of the ketogenic diet has to do with the low levels of insulin in the body, which causes greater lipolysis and free-glycerol release compared to a normal diet when insulin is around 80-120.

TIPS TO GET YOU STARTED ON THE KITOGENIC DIET

1. Make sure you choose a low-carb diet plan.
2. Make sure you eat real food when you hungry.
3. Always measuring progress wisely and thinking long-term.
4. Make sure you avoid alcohol, fruit and artificial sweeteners, while you eat less dairy and nut products, stocking up on vitamins and minerals.
5. Make sure you review your medications, stressing less and sleeping more.
6. Finally, always exercise your body.

Mustard Balsamic Baked Chicken Recipe

Ingredients
2 tablespoons of Dijon (or homemade mustard)
1 cup of olive oil
4 tablespoons of fresh rosemary (minced)
Sea salt and freshly ground black pepper to taste
16 boneless chicken thighs
½ cup of balsamic vinegar
4 tablespoons of fresh lemon juice
2-garlic cloves (minced)

Directions:
1. First, you combine the mustard, balsamic vinegar, garlic, rosemary, lemon juice, in a bowl, and season to taste with salt and pepper.

2. After which you slowly pour the olive oil in with the mixture while whisking.

3. After that, you place the chicken in a marinating container (preferably, glass or plastic; do not use metal) and pour the mustard balsamic marinade on top.

4. At this point, you place in the refrigerator or leave on the counter, covered, and marinate for about 30 minutes.

5. Meanwhile, you heat your oven to temperature of 375 F.

6. Then you transfer the chicken to a baking dish and empty the remaining sauce on top.

7. This is when you place in the oven and bake for about an hour or until the chicken is cooked.

8. Make sure you serve with roasted vegetables.

Nutrition Information
Amount per serving
Calories: 210
Fat: 9.8g
Protein: 26.0g
Dietary Fiber: 0.5g
Carbohydrates: 3.1g

Skillet Rosemary Chicken Recipe

Ingredients
40oz (about 2lbs) mixed mushrooms, cut in half
2 tablespoons of fresh rosemary leave, minced
4 lemons
Sea salt and freshly ground black pepper to taste
8-12, bone-in chicken thighs, skin on or off
4 sprigs fresh rosemary
6 cloves garlic, minced
4 tablespoons of extra-virgin olive oil;

Directions:
1. Meanwhile, you heat your oven to a temperature of 450F.

2. After which you mix up the rosemary-garlic vinaigrette in a bowl by combining the minced rosemary, garlic, olive oil, juice of 2 lemons.

3. After that, you season with salt and pepper to taste.

4. At this point, you coat each chicken piece with the vinaigrette.

5. Then you heat an oven-safe skillet over a medium-high and sear the chicken, skin-side down, for about 5 minutes until browned.

6. Furthermore, you remove the chicken from pan and add the mushrooms.

7. After which you return the chicken to the pan on top of the mushrooms and drizzle with the remaining vinaigrette and the juice from the other lemon.

8. Then you add the rosemary sprig and the squeezed lemon halves to the skillet and place in the oven.

9. Finally, you roast for about 20 to 25 min.

Nutrition Information
Amount per serving 1(357)
Calories: 436.5
Fat: 22.7g
Protein: 39.0g
Dietary Fiber: 2.0g
Carbohydrates: 18.7g

Coconut-Buttermilk Southwestern Grilled

Ingredients
6 cloves garlic (minced)
4 teaspoons of ground coriander
2 teaspoons of turmeric
Sea salt and freshly ground black pepper to taste
4 lbs. of chicken parts (such as thighs, drumsticks, legs, etc.)
4 tablespoons of chili powder
4 teaspoons of ground cumin
Fresh cilantro, it is optional
Zest and juice of 2 limes;
Ingredients for the coconut buttermilk
4 tablespoons of lemon juice
4 cups of coconut milk

Directions:
1. First, you combine the coconut milk and lemon juice in a bowl.

2. After which, you mix well and let it sit for about 5 minutes.

3. After that, you add the chili powder, turmeric, garlic, coriander, cumin, lime zest, and lime juice to the coconut buttermilk mixture.

4. Then you season to taste and mix thoroughly.

5. At this point, you pour the marinade over the chicken and refrigerate for about 4 to 12 hours.

6. Meanwhile, you heat a grill to a medium-heat.

7. After which you remove the chicken from the marinade and grill for about 15 to 20 minutes total until cooked through and golden on both sides.

8. Finally, you sprinkle with fresh cilantro to serve.

Nutrition Information
Amount per serving 1(66g)
Calories: 132.8
Fat: 6.7g
Protein: 3.9g
Dietary Fiber: 2.3g

Slow Cooker Chipotle Barbacoa Brisket

Ingredients:
1 to 2 cups of my Chipotle Adobo Sauce (or 6 chipotles from a can plus 6 tablespoons of sauce)
2 small white onions (diced)
4 teaspoons of oregano
4 bay leaves
2 (2.5 to 4 pound) beef brisket
4 cups of beef stock
6 large cloves of garlic
1 teaspoon of ground cloves
2 tablespoons of apple cider vinegar

Directions:
1. First, you make a liquid puree with all of your ingredients except the beef or the bay leaves.

2. After which you pour about a quarter of your liquid puree into the bottom of your slow cooker.

3. After that, you trim any excessive fat from your brisket and place it in your slow cooker fat cap side down.

4. Remember that you do not need a lot of fat on your brisket at all.

5. At this point, you pour the rest of your liquid puree over your brisket ensuring that you coat the top sides.

6. Then you cook on low for about 8 hours.

7. Furthermore, you remove your brisket to a large bowl or container to pull/shred with 2 forks.

8. After which you add some of the cooking liquid from the crock-pot to your pulled brisket.

9. Serve in lettuce wrap tacos, with your eggs, over salads, or just by pulling strips off and feeding your face!

Nutrition Information
Amount per serving 1(272)
Calories: 362.2
Fat: 17.5g
Protein: 48.7g
Dietary Fiber: 0.3g
Carbohydrates: 2.6g

Rosemary Ranch Chicken Kabobs Recipe

Ingredients
1 cup of olive oil
4 tablespoons of coconut aminos
2 teaspoons of fresh lemon juice
Wood skewers
8 skinless, boneless chicken breasts (cut into 1-inch pieces)
1 cup of homemade ranch dressing (see directions below)
2 tablespoons of fresh rosemary (minced)
2 teaspoons of balsamic vinegar
Sea salt and freshly ground black pepper to taste
Ingredients for ranch dressing
1 cup of coconut milk
2 garlic cloves (minced)
Salt and freshly ground pepper, to taste
1 cup of homemade mayonnaise
1 teaspoon of onion powder
2 teaspoons of fresh dill (minced)

Directions:
1. First, you whisk all the ingredients for the ranch dressing together in a bowl until well combined.

2. After which you season to taste with salt and pepper.

3. After that, you combine the olive oil, ranch dressing, coconut aminos, rosemary, lemon juice, balsamic vinegar, in a large bowl and season with salt and pepper to taste.

4. Then you add the chicken to the bowl, and stir until well coated.

5. At this point, you place the bowl in the refrigerator and let it sit for at least 30 minutes.

6. Meanwhile, you heat your grill to a medium-high heat.

7. Then you thread the chicken cubes onto the skewers.

8. Finally, you grill the skewers on each side until the chicken is cooked through, about 10 to 12 minutes in total.

9. Make sure you serve warm.

Nutrition Information
Amount per serving 1(187)
Calories: 350.7
Fat: 21.8g
Protein: 31.3g
Dietary Fiber: 0.1g
Carbohydrates: 5.9g

Chicken and Pineapple Skewers Recipe

Ingredients
½ cup of honey
4 garlic cloves (minced)
8 boneless, skinless chicken breasts (cut into cubes)
Sea salt and freshly ground black pepper to taste
2 cups of homemade ketchup
2 tablespoons of Dijon mustard
Juice of two lemons
2 fresh pineapples (peeled and cut into chunks)
32 wooden skewers (soaked in water)

Directions:
1. First, you combine the ketchup, honey, mustard, garlic, and lemon juice in a saucepan placed over a medium heat.

2. After which you bring to a simmer, cook until thick, and set aside.

3. Meanwhile, you heat a grill to a medium-high heat.

4. At this point, you thread alternating pieces of chicken and pineapple onto the skewers.

5. After that, you season skewers with salt and pepper.

6. After which you pour about half the sauce into a bowl, and brush the skewers with some of the remaining sauce.

7. Then you cook the skewers on the grill, basting regularly with the barbecue sauce for about 10 minutes, until cooked through.

8. Finally, you serve with the remaining barbecue sauce.

Nutrition Information
Amount per serving 1(138g)
Calories: 221
Fat: 6.4g
Protein: 25.2g

Chicken Drumsticks with Orange Glaze

Ingredients
3 cloves garlic (minced)
One-star anise
1 cup of fresh orange juice;
3 tablespoons of coconut aminos
1 tablespoons of raw honey (it is optional)
Sea salt and freshly ground black pepper to taste
Twelve chicken drumsticks
2 tablespoons of fresh ginger (grated)
2 cinnamon sticks (broken in half)
The Zest of one orange
1 tablespoon of white rice vinegar
4 green onions (chopped)

Directions:
1. First, you add all the ingredients, except the drumsticks, to a saucepan placed over a medium-high heat.

2. After which you season to taste with salt and pepper.

3. After that, you bring to a simmer and then lower the heat and let simmer for about 15 to 20 minutes or until the sauce thickens.

4. At this point, you set the sauce aside and let it cool down.

5. Then you place the chicken in a marinating container (preferably, a glass or plastic) and pour sauce on top, making sure that every piece coats well.

6. Furthermore, you marinate in the refrigerator for at least 2 hours.

7. Meanwhile, you heat your oven to a temperature of 425 F.

8. Then you arrange the drumsticks on a baking pan and place them in the oven.

9. Finally, you bake for about 40 to 45 minutes, basting every 15 minutes with the remaining sauce.

Nutrition Information
Amount per serving 1(168g)
Calories: 291.7
Fat: 10.6g
Protein: 23.5g
Dietary Fiber: 0.6g

Sweet Garlic Chicken Recipe

Ingredients
½ cup of raw honey (it is optional)
4 tablespoons of fresh lemon juice
4 tablespoons of coconut aminos
4 tablespoons of water
Sea salt and freshly ground black pepper to taste
8 chicken breasts
½ cup of apple cider vinegar
6 tablespoons of garlic (minced)
4 teaspoons of tapioca starch (it is optional)
Red pepper flakes (to taste)

Directions:
1. First, you place the chicken in your slow cooker.

2. After which you combine the honey, vinegar, lemon juice, garlic, coconut aminos and water in a bowl.

3. After that, you season to taste with salt and pepper.

4. At this point, you pour the sauce over the chicken, cover, and cook on low for about 6 to 8 hours.

5. Then you take the chicken out of the slow cooker and pour the sauce into a saucepan.

6. This is when you warm-up the sauce over medium-high heat.

7. After which you combine 4 teaspoons of water with the tapioca starch and add to the sauce.

8. After that, you let the sauce come to a boil and stir until it thickens.

9. Finally, you sprinkle some red pepper flakes over the chicken and pour the sauce on top.

10. When serving, feel free to serve on a bed of your favorite steamed vegetables.

Nutrition Information
Amount per serving 1(138g)
Calories: 221.2
Fat: 6.4g
Protein: 25.2g
Carbohydrates: 14.5g

Slow Cooker Buffalo Chicken Meatballs

Ingredients
2/3 cup of almond meal
4 cloves garlic (minced)
1 ¼ cup of buffalo sauce
Sea salt and freshly ground black pepper to taste
2 lbs. ground chicken
2 eggs
4 green onions (thinly sliced)
Homemade ranch dressing (it is optional)

Directions:
1. Meanwhile, you heat your oven to a temperature of 400 degrees F.

2. After which you combine the ground chicken, almond meal, egg, garlic, green onions, in a bowl and season with salt and pepper to taste.

3. After that, you mix everything until well combined.

4. At this point, you roll the mixture into 1 ½ -inch meatballs.

5. Then you place the meatballs onto a baking sheet and bake for about 5 minutes in the preheated oven.

6. This is the point when you turn off the oven and place meatballs into a slow cooker.

7. Furthermore, you add the buffalo sauce, and stir to combine.

8. Then you cover and cook on low for about 2 hours.

9. Finally, you serve with ranch sauce for dipping (it is optional).

Nutrition Information
Amount per serving 1(244)
Calories: 281
Fat: 7.9g
Protein: 32.9g
Dietary Fiber: 1.6g

Slow Cooker Queso Chicken Chili Recipe

Ingredients
4 ½ bell peppers (minced)
1 ½ jalapeño pepper, minced (it is optional)
3 garlic cloves (minced)
1 ½ teaspoons of ground cumin
Sea salt and freshly ground black pepper to taste
1 ½ lbs. of boneless skinless chicken breasts
1 ½ red onions (chopped)
3 cups of salsa
2 ½-cups of water
3 teaspoons of chili powder
2 avocados (chopped)

Directions:
1. First, you combine the chicken breasts, garlic, salsa, water, cumin, chili powder, onion, in a slow cooker, and season with salt and pepper to taste.

2. After which you cover and cook on low for about 6 to 8 hours (or on high for about 3-4 hours).

3. Once the cooking is done, you remove the chicken breasts and shred them with a fork, after which you return them to the slow cooker.

4. After that, you place the bell peppers and jalapeño in a large skillet over a high heat and cook for about 4 to 5 minutes or until well roasted.

5. Then you add the peppers and jalapeño to the slow cooker.

6. At this point, you give everything a good stir and cover.

7. After which you let the chili simmer for another 20 minutes, and add some water to reach the desired consistency, if needed.

8. Make sure you top with avocado before serving.

Nutrition Information
Amount per serving 1(88g)
Calories: 168.8
Fat: 13.6g
Protein: 8.6g
Carbohydrates: 3.2g

Meat loaf with mushrooms recipe

Ingredients
1 ½ teaspoons of sea salt
An egg
2 cups of white button mushrooms (finely chopped)
3 teaspoons of fresh thyme (minced)
3 cloves garlic (minced)
1 tablespoons of honey (it is optional)
1 tablespoons of paleo cooking fat
2 lbs. of ground beef (feel free to substitute with ground pork)
1 teaspoon of ground black pepper to taste
1 medium onion (finely chopped)
½ tablespoons of Worcestershire sauce (it is optional)
1 teaspoon of fresh oregano (minced)
½ cup of homemade ketchup
1 teaspoon of chili pepper flakes

Directions:
1. Meanwhile, you heat your oven to a temperature of 350 F.

2. After which you use a medium sized skillet placed over a medium heat, to melt the cooking fat, add the mushrooms and sauté for about 2 to 3 minutes, or until soft.

3. After that, you combine the meat, salt, pepper, egg, onion, mushrooms, chili pepper, thyme, oregano and garlic in a large bowl.

4. At this point, you mix well, making sure to break-up the meat.

5. Then you add the cooked mushrooms as well.

6. Make sure that the mushrooms are distributed evenly to ensure the loaf bonds well.

7. This is when you lightly grease loaf pan with additional cooking fat and fill it with the meat mixture.

8. After that, you place in the oven and cook for approximately 15 minutes.

9. Meanwhile, you combine ketchup, honey and Worcestershire sauce in a small bowl, to make the sauce for the top of the meatloaf.

10. After you might have cooked it for 15 minutes, you gently spread the sauce on the top of the loaf.

11. Then you continue cooking for another 40 minutes.

Nutrition Information
Amount per serving 1(443g)
Calories: 620.1
Fat: 37.9g
Protein: 41.4g
Dietary Fiber: 3.4g
Carbohydrates: 26.1g

Bean less chili recipe

Ingredients
7 ½ lbs. of ground beef
9 cloves garlic (minced)
7 ½ celery stalks (chopped)
6 cups of button mushrooms (chopped)
4 ½ thyme sprigs
Sea salt and freshly ground black pepper to taste
4 ½ quarts good quality canned tomatoes
1 ½ tablespoons of extra-virgin olive oil
1 ½ onions (finely chopped)
7 ½ carrots (chopped)
4 ½ bay leaves
3 tablespoons of fresh parsley (chopped)

Directions:
1. First, you cook the ground beef with some cooking fat if needed in a large skillet over a medium heat.

2. After which you use a very large saucepan sauté the garlic in olive oil over a medium heat.

3. After that, you cook for about 2 minutes, or until the garlic is fragrant.

4. At this point, you add the onion, celery, carrots and mushrooms to the saucepan.

5. Then you stir well and cook for another 5 to 10 minutes, until the vegetables are soft.

6. This is when you add the canned tomatoes, followed by the cooked ground beef and then stir thoroughly.

7. Furthermore, you drop in the bay leaves, thyme and parsley.

8. After which you season to taste with salt and pepper, reduce the heat to low and simmer, uncovered, for approximately 4 hours or until thick, stirring occasionally.

9. After that, you adjust the seasoning by adding salt or pepper, if needed.

10. Finally, you remove the bay leaves and thyme sprigs.

Nutrition Information
Amount per serving ()
Calories: 196.5
Fat: 12.6g
Protein: 12.3g
Dietary Fiber: 3.1g
Carbohydrates: 10g

Hearty beef stew recipe

Ingredients
4 tablespoons of paleo cooking fat
2 cups of onion (chopped)
6 carrots (peeled and chopped)
2 (28oz) can diced tomatoes
Sea salt and freshly ground black pepper to taste
2 lbs. of stewing beef
8 cups of beef stock
2 cups of celery (chopped)
4 potatoes, peeled and cubed (it is optional)
1 teaspoon of fresh rosemary (finely chopped)
1 teaspoon of fresh thyme (finely chopped)

Directions:
1. First, you combine the onions, celery, carrots, potatoes, if using, as well as the cooking fat in a large saucepan over a medium-high heat.

2. After which you cook for about 3 to 5 minutes, stirring constantly.

3. After that, you add the beef to the saucepan, followed by the tomatoes, beef stock, rosemary and thyme.

4. At this point, you season to taste with salt and pepper.

5. Then you cover the saucepan and cook for about one hour, allowing the stew to simmer.

6. This is when you stir a few times during the cooking process.

7. Finally, you remove the lid and cook uncovered for about 45 minutes and if the mixture is too thick at the end of the cooking process, I suggest you add a little bit of water or stock.

Nutrition Information
Amount per serving 1(285g)
Calories: 262.6
Fat: 4.3g
Protein: 27.0g
Dietary Fiber: 3.0g

Roast beef with thyme, garlic and red wine

Ingredients
1 cup of clarified butter (or beef tallow)
6 cloves garlic (minced)
Sea salt and freshly ground black pepper to taste
2 (4lbs) top sirloin roast
6 tablespoons of homemade Worcestershire sauce (it is optional)
6 sprigs fresh thyme
1 ¼ cups of red wine

Directions:
1. Meanwhile, you heat your oven to a temperature of 350 F.

2. After which you melt 2 tablespoons of the cooking fat in a large skillet over high heat.

3. After that, you sear the roast on all sides for just a few moments, or until the sides are a beautiful golden brown.

4. Then you place the roast in a large roasting dish, along with the cooking fat used to sear it.

5. At this point, you scatter generous knobs of the cooking fat on top of the roast, followed by the Worcestershire sauce, if using, and red wine.

6. Furthermore, you sprinkle the garlic over the meat and season to taste with salt and pepper.

7. After which you top with the thyme sprigs.

8. After that, you allow to cook for about 50-60 minutes, or until the meat is cooked, but still slightly pink in the middle.

9. This is the point when you baste the meat with the cooking juices from time to time during the cooking process to ensure that the meat stays moist.

10. Then you remove the roast from the oven and set aside for about 10 minutes before serving, allowing the meat to relax before carving it.

11. Finally, you remove the thyme springs from the pan and use the rendered liquid in the pan as a sauce for the roast.

Nutrition Information
Amount per serving ()
Calories: 441
Fat: 31.9g
Protein: 30.6g
Dietary Fiber: 0.1g
Carbohydrates: 3.5g

Bacon-wrapped mini meatloaves Recipe

Ingredients
1lb. of bacon (cut in small chunks)
½ cup of coconut milk
2/3 cup of fresh chives (minced)
Freshly ground black pepper to taste
2 lbs. of ground beef
16 additional strips of bacons
4 garlic cloves (minced)
Fresh parsley (chopped)

Directions:
1. Meanwhile, you heat your oven to a temperature of 400 F.

2. After which you combine the ground beef, the bacon chunks, the garlic, the chives and the coconut Milk in a big bowl.

3. After that, you mix well until all the ingredients hold together. To save yourself some time, I suggest you use an electric mixer.

4. At this point, you season the mixture with freshly ground black pepper to taste. Do not add salt to the mixture since the bacon is already salty enough.

5. Then you take a medium size muffin tin and place a slice of bacon around the sides of each hole.

6. Furthermore, you fill these same eight holes with the beef mixture.

7. After that, you place in the oven and cook for about 30 minutes.

8. Then once it is ready and cool enough to handle, you remove the mini meatloaves from the muffin tin and serve with fresh parsley sprinkled on top.

Nutrition Information
Amount per serving 1(118g)
Calories: 213.6
Fat: 12.2g
Protein: 17.9g
Dietary Fiber: 0.4g
Carbohydrates: 6.9g

Sirloin Steak with Avocado Salad Recipe

Ingredients
2 avocados (peeled and diced)
1 cup of celery (sliced)
4 tablespoons of extra virgin olive oil
Sea salt and freshly ground black pepper to taste
4 big sirloin steaks
2 big red bell pepper (diced)
4 green onions (chopped)
2 tablespoons of lemon juice
4 tablespoons of Paleo cooking fat

Directions:
1. First, you use a skillet big enough to cook two steaks, melt 2 tablespoons of the cooking fat over medium-high heat.

2. After which you cook the red bell peppers for about 2 to 3 minutes until soft but still crunchy and set aside.

3. After that, you season the 4 steaks with sea salt and freshly ground black pepper to taste.

4. Then you use the same skillet, add the cooking fat and brown the two sirloins on each side, until done to your liking. Have in mind that in 2-3 minutes on each side will give you a nice medium-rare steak.

5. At this point, you remove the steaks from the skillet and let them rest for about 5 minutes.

6. This is when you combine the roasted red bell peppers, the green onions, the avocado, the celery, the lemon juice, and the olive oil, to prepare the salad in a big bowl.

7. After that, you season to taste with sea salt and freshly ground black pepper.

8. Finally, you cut the steak into slices, and serve with the avocado salad on top.

Nutrition Information
Amount per serving 1(3089)
Calories: 366.4
Fat: 24.0g
Protein: 26.6g
Dietary Fiber: 2.9g
Carbohydrates: 11.4g

Grilled Steak and Summer Veggies Recipe

Ingredients
Four small zucchini (cut lengthwise)
2 cups of grape tomatoes (halved)
Fresh Herbs Vinaigrette
1 ½ lbs. of beef flank steak
½ cup of red onions (chopped)
4 big carrots (cut lengthwise)
Ingredients
½ cup of fresh basil (chopped)
1 teaspoons of Dijon mustard
Sea salt and freshly ground black pepper to taste
½ cup of fresh parsley (chopped)
1 clove garlic (chopped)
6 tablespoons of extra virgin olive oil
Juice from ½ a lemon

Directions:
1. First, you combine the entire ingredients for the vinaigrette except for the olive oil in a food processor.

2. After which you blend the entire ingredients for one minute, and then slowly pour in the olive oil.

3. At this point, you transfer to a bowl and reserve.

4. Meanwhile, you heat the grill to a medium-high heat.

5. After which you grill the flank steak for about 8 minutes for medium rare or more if you like it well done.

6. At a point, once it is cooked, you remove from the grill and set aside to rest.

7. After that, you combine the zucchini, the carrots, the red onions and 1 tablespoons of the vinaigrette and combine well.

8. Then you place the vegetables on the grill and cook for about 5 to 6 minutes, flipping them once.

9. Furthermore, you cut the cooked steak into slices and, in a big bowl, combine the steak, the cooked vegetables, and the grape tomatoes.

10. Finally, you add the remaining vinaigrette and toss to mix.

11. After which you season to taste with sea salt and black pepper before serving.

Veal Chops with Rosemary Recipe

Ingredients
6 cloves garlic (minced)
4 tablespoons of Paleo cooking fat
Sea salt and freshly ground black pepper to taste
4 veal chops
4 tablespoons of fresh rosemary (minced)
1 cup of white wine (it is optional)
½ cup of chicken stock

Directions:
1. Meanwhile, you heat your oven to a temperature of 350 F.

2. After which you rub the chops with rosemary and garlic on each side and season to taste; then let them rest for 10 minutes.

3. After that, you warm the cooking fat in a skillet placed over a medium high heat.

4. Cook the chops in the skillet for about 5 to 7 minutes on each side until golden brown.

5. At this point, you transfer the chops from the skillet to a baking dish, and bake in the oven for 10 more minutes.

6. In the meanwhile, over a medium heat, you add the wine and chicken stock to the previously used skillet, and warm everything up for about a minute or two.

7. Then you scrape off any flakes of food on the bottom of the pan while the liquid is warming up.

8. Finally, you remove the chops from the oven, top with the sauce, and serve.

Nutrition Information
Amount per serving 1(106)
Calories: 183.9
Fat: 13.9g
Protein: 1.0g
Dietary Fiber: 0.1g
Carbohydrates: 3.7g

Beef Brisket with Fall Vegetables Recipe

Ingredients
4 carrots (cut into 2-inch pieces)
2 celery ribs (sliced)
1 leek (sliced)
2 cups of beef stock (preferably, 3 cups if not using wine)
½ cups of tomato puree
8 garlic cloves (minced)
Sea Salt and freshly ground black pepper to taste
2 lbs. of beef brisket
4 parsnips (sliced)
1 large onion (sliced)
6 fresh thyme sprigs
¾ cup of dry red wine (it is optional)
2 tablespoons of Beau Monde seasoning (see directions below, but it is optional)
¾ cup of fresh parsley (chopped)
Cooking fat

Ingredients for the Beau Monde Seasoning
1 tablespoon of ground cloves
1 teaspoons of ground cinnamon
1 tablespoons of ground bay leaf
1 tablespoons of ground allspice
1 teaspoons of ground nutmeg
1 teaspoon of celery seed
Sea salt and freshly ground black pepper to taste

Directions:
1. First, you combine the entire ingredients for the Beau Monde seasoning in a small bowl.

2. After which you sprinkle beef with salt and pepper to taste.

3. After which you heat some cooking fat over a medium-high heat in a large skillet and brown the beef on each side for about 4 minutes.

4. At this point, you transfer beef to a slow cooker.

5. Then you add the carrot, parsnips, celery, onion, and leek.

6. Furthermore, you mix the beef stock, red wine (if using), tomato puree, garlic, thyme sprigs, parsley, and Beau Monde seasoning in a bowl.

7. After which you pour the mixture over the beef and vegetables.

8. Then you cover and cook on low for about 10 to 12 hours or until tender.

9. Finally, you serve warm with the vegetables.

Nutrition Information
Amount per serving 1(685)
Calories: 956
Fat: 58.4g
Protein: 61.6g
Dietary Fiber: 12g

Salmon tartare with fresh herbs recipe

Ingredients
2 tablespoons of chives (minced)
1 red onion (minced)
2-4 tablespoons of capers
Juice from 2 fresh lemons
Sea salt and freshly ground black pepper to taste
2 lbs. of wild salmon filet (skinless)
2 tablespoons of fresh basil (minced)
4 green onions (minced)
½ cup of extra-virgin olive oil
2 tablespoons of Dijon (or homemade mustard)

Directions:
1. First, you cut the salmon filet into small cubes of about ¼ inches.

2. After which you store in the refrigerator.

3. After that, you combine all the herbs and vegetables in a small bowl: the chives, basil, red onion, capers and green onions.

4. Then you add the olive oil, the mustard and the lemon juice in a big bowl.

5. At this point, you combine well with a whisk.

6. Furthermore, you add the herbs and vegetables to the vinaigrette and combine well.

7. After which you add the salmon to the bowl and combine well again.

8. Then you season with sea salt and freshly ground black pepper to taste.

9. After that, you place the bowl in the freezer for about 15 to 20 minutes, until very cold, but not frozen.

10. Finally, you place in small bowls to serve and add some fresh herbs on top to create a great presentation

Nutrition Information
Amount per serving ()
Calories: 298
Fat: 23.5g
Protein: 18.4g
Dietary Fiber: 0.3g
Carbohydrates: 3.2g

Tuna Burger Recipe

Ingredients
4 scallions (thinly sliced)
½ cup of homemade mayonnaise
Extra-virgin olive oil (for brushing)
Sea salt and freshly ground black pepper, to taste
2 lbs. fresh tuna (diced)
24 Kalamata olives (pitted and chopped)
2 teaspoons of anchovy paste
Sliced tomatoes and arugula, to serve

Directions:
1. Meanwhile, you heat your grill to medium high.

2. After which you combine the tuna, the Kalamata olives, and the scallions in a bowl.

3. After that, you place the mixture in the freezer for about 5 minutes.

4. At this point when the 5 minutes is up, you transfer the tuna mixture into a food processor and pulse until the tuna is finely chopped.

5. Then you transfer back to the bowl and season to taste.

6. Furthermore, you flatten the tuna into 8 patties of equal size.

7. After which you brush each patty with olive oil and grill for about 6 to 8 minutes total, flipping once.

8. After that, you combine the mayonnaise with the anchovy paste in a small bowl.

9. Finally, you spread the mayonnaise and anchovy paste on each tuna patty.

10. Then you top with tomato and arugula and serve.

Nutrition Information
Amount per serving ()
Calories: 90
Fat: 0.5g
Protein: 19g
Carbohydrates: 3.0g

Salmon Florentine Recipe

Ingredients
10 oz. of fresh spinach
4 garlic cloves (minced)
¼ teaspoons of red pepper flakes
Coconut oil
4 skinless salmon fillets, 6 oz. each (rinsed and patted dry)
¼ cup of shallots (minced)
5 sun-dried tomatoes (chopped)
Sea salt and freshly ground black pepper to taste to taste

Directions:
1. Meanwhile, you heat your oven to a temperature of 350 F.

2. After which you heat the coconut oil in a skillet placed over a medium heat.

3. After that, you add the shallots and cook for about 3 minutes, until soft, stirring occasionally.

4. Then you add the garlic and cook for another minute.

5. At this point, you add the spinach, sun-dried tomatoes, and pepper flakes and then cook for another 2 to 3 minutes and season to taste.

6. This is when you remove the vegetables from the heat and set aside.

7. After which you season each salmon filet with salt, pepper to taste, and line them up in a baking dish.

8. After that, you top each filet with the spinach mixture and place in the oven.

9. Finally, you bake for about 15 to 20 minutes or until the fish is just cooked through.

Nutrition Information
Amount per serving 1(523)
Calories: 506
Fat: 18.0g
Protein: 73.7g
Dietary Fiber: 5.2g
Carbohydrates: 12g

Grilled Shrimp Skewers with Watermelon and Avocado Recipe

Ingredients
2 avocadoes (peeled, pitted, and cut into cubes)
2-jalapeño pepper (stem removed)
2 (1-inch) piece fresh ginger, peeled
2/3 cup of fresh mint
16 bamboo skewers (soaked for an hour)
48 shrimp (peeled and deveined)
6 cups of seedless watermelon (cut into cubes)
2 large garlic clove
2-cup coconut milk
½ cup of fresh lime juice
2 tablespoons of fish sauce;

Directions:
1. First, you blend the jalapeño, garlic, ginger, coconut milk, fresh mint, lime juice, and fish sauce in a food processor, on high speed until smooth to make the marinade.

2. After which you mix the shrimp with marinade in a bowl, cover, and refrigerate for an hour.

3. Meanwhile, you heat your grill to a medium-high heat.

4. After that, you remove the shrimp from the marinade.

5. Then you thread the shrimp on skewers with the avocado and watermelon.

6. At this point, you place the skewers on the preheated grill for about 6 to 8 minutes, turning once.

7. Make sure you serve warm.

Nutrition Information
Amount per serving ()
Calories: 223
Fat: 8g
Protein: 24.5g
Dietary Fiber: 3g

Shrimp Burgers with Pineapple-Avocado

Ingredients
4 tablespoons of cilantro (coarsely chopped)
2-garlic clove (minced)
½ cup of celery (minced)
2 tablespoons of lemon juice
Sea salt and freshly ground black pepper to taste
3 lb. of shrimp (any size, peeled, and deveined)
4 tablespoons of fresh chives
½ cup of radishes (minced)
2 teaspoons of fresh lemon zest
2 eggs, beaten
½ cup of almond meal
Ingredients for the Pineapple-Avocado Salsa
2 avocados (pitted, peeled, and diced)
4 tablespoons of red onion (finely diced)
Sea salt and freshly ground black pepper to taste
2 cups of fresh pineapple (finely chopped)
½ cup of bell peppers (finely chopped)
2 tablespoons of fresh lime juice
2 tablespoons of chopped cilantro

Directions:
1. First, you combine the entire ingredients for the salsa in a bowl and refrigerate.

2. Meanwhile, you heat your grill to a medium-high heat.

3. After which you combine the shrimp, cilantro, chives, and garlic in a food processor.

4. After that, you pulse until the shrimp are finely chopped.

5. Then you combine the shrimp mixture with the radish, celery, almond meal, beaten egg, lemon zest, and lemon juice in a large bowl.

6. At this point, you season to taste with salt and pepper.

7. Furthermore, you shape the mixture into 4 burger patties.

8. After which you grill each burger for about 4 to 5 minutes per side, or until cooked through.

9. Finally, you serve the burgers with salsa spooned over top.

Bacon-Wrapped Salmon Recipe

Ingredients
4 sprigs of tarragon (cut in half)
16 slices of bacon
Sea Salt and freshly ground pepper to taste
8 wild salmon fillets, about 10 oz. each (that is just a total of less than 4 lbs. of salmon)
Zest of two lemons
4 tablespoons of maple syrup or raw honey (it is optional)
Cooking fat

Directions:
1. Meanwhile, you heat your oven to a temperature of 375 F.

2. After which you season the salmon to taste with sea salt and freshly ground black pepper.

3. After that, you top each fillet with a sprig of tarragon and some lemon zest.

4. Then you wrap each fillet with two slices of bacon.

5. At this point, you heat some cooking fat in a large ovenproof skillet over a medium-high heat.

6. After which you fry the salmon on each side until golden brown (at approximately 2 minutes per side).

7. This is when you brush each fillet with the maple syrup or honey, if using, and transfer to the oven.

8. Finally, you place the salmon in the oven until cooked through (at approximately8 to 10 minutes).

**Nutrition Information
Amount per serving ()**
Calories: 423
Fat: 29g
Protein: 39g
Carbohydrates: 1g

Bigos Recipe

Ingredients
6 cups of sauerkraut
¾ lb. of bacon sliced
1 ½ lbs. of Kielbasa sausage sliced (it is optionally substitute with a quality sausage from your butcher)
3 cloves garlic (minced)
Salt and pepper to taste (it is optional)
¾ medium cabbage
1 ½-can tomato paste
1 ½ lbs. of pork diced (note that any parts that can be sautéed is good)
1 ½ large onion (diced)
1 ½ bay leaf

Directions:
1. First, you cut your washed cabbage in thin slice and boil until tender in a pot.

2. After which you boil the sauerkraut in another pot in about 3 cups of water.

3. After that, you strain and keep the sour water aside.

4. At this point, you sauté your diced pork in a pan with some cooking oil (lard, coconut oil or butter are good).

5. Then you set aside and sauté the bacon and sausage with the onion and garlic.

6. Furthermore, you combine the cooked cabbage, sauerkraut, sour water, tomato paste, spices and your cooked meats, onion and garlic in a large pot.

7. Finally, you let simmer for about an hour.

Nutrition Information
Amount per serving 1(451g)
Calories: 352.3
Fat: 21.2g
Protein: 23.5g
Dietary Fiber: 7.1g
Carbohydrates: 18.5g

Thai Pork Lettuce Wraps Recipe

Ingredients
2 cups of chicken stock
A Fresh lettuce leaves (cut into approximately 3 x 3 inches)
1 tablespoons of fish sauce
4 tablespoons of water
1 lime (quartered)
Sea salt and freshly ground black pepper to taste
1 lb. pork, thinly sliced
¾ lb. of mung bean sprouts
½ cup of almond butter
2 tablespoons of white wine vinegar
1 teaspoon of sambal sauce (it is optional)
1 tablespoon of Paleo cooking fat;

Directions:
1. First, you bring the chicken stock to a boil in a pan placed over a medium-high heat and add the pork slices.

2. After which you simmer and cook for about 5 minutes, until the pork is cooked.

3. After that, you remove the pork pieces and set aside to cool (Note: you will not need the chicken stock anymore, but you can stock it in the refrigerator for later recipes).

4. At this point, you cook the mung bean sprouts with the cooking fat in the same pan, for about 3 to 4 minutes and then set aside.

5. Then you combine the ingredients for the almond butter sauce in a bowl: the almond butter, fish sauce, white wine vinegar, and water and sambal sauce.

6. Season it with sea salt and black pepper to taste.

7. Furthermore, once the cooked ingredients have cooled down, you place some pork; some mung bean sprouts and some almond butter sauce over each lettuce leave and then squeeze some fresh lime juice on top.

8. Finally, you roll them into wraps and enjoy.

Nutrition Information
Amount per serving 1(164g)
Calories: 176.8
Fat: 4.3g
Protein: 25.5g
Dietary Fiber: 2.1g
Carbohydrates: 9.4g

Pork Chop with Peaches Recipe

Ingredients
4 green onions (thinly sliced)
4 peaches (cut into 16 wedges)
1cup of chicken stock
Sea salt and freshly ground black pepper to taste
8 boneless pork chops
2 tablespoons of fresh thyme (chopped)
1 cup of dry white wine
4 teaspoons of ghee (or preferable other Paleo cooking fat)
4 teaspoons of olive oil;

Directions:
1. First, you heat a large skillet over a medium-high heat and add the olive oil.

2. After which you season the chops with sea salt and freshly ground black pepper, and add them to the skillet.

3. After that, you cook on both sides until done (for about 6 minute's total, 3 minutes on each side).

4. At this point, you remove the chops from the pan, and keep them warm.

5. Then you add the green onions, thyme, peaches to the pan, and cook for about 2 minutes.

6. Furthermore, you stir in the wine and bring to a boil until reduced by almost half.

7. After that, stir in the chicken stock and bring to a boil.

8. After which you simmer until reduced by half once again.

9. Then you remove the pan from the heat and stir in the ghee until dissolved.

10. Finally, you drizzle the sauce over the chops and serve.

Nutrition Information
Amount per serving 1(324g)
Calories: 397.1
Fat: 23.3g
Protein: 35.5g
Dietary Fiber: 2.1g
Carbohydrates: 10.5g

Homemade Ham Recipe

Ingredients
Water
½ cup of honey
2 tablespoons of pickling spice
8-10 lbs. of pork leg
1 cup of sea salt
8 tablespoons of curing salt (Prague Powder #1)

Directions:
1. First, you place the pork in a bowl large enough to fit the ham and fill it with water.

2. After which you add the salt, curing salt, honey, and pickling spice.

3. After that, you give everything a good stir, cover, and place in the refrigerator for about 4 to 5 days (1 day per pound of ham) to brine.

4. At a point, when the ham is done brining, you remove from the bowl and rinse off.

5. Then you place the pork in a big saucepan filled with water and bring to a boil over a medium heat.

6. Let simmer for approximately 25 minutes per pound or until the interior reaches a temperature of 155 F.

7. Finally, you let everything cool down which will take 30 minutes, after cooking.

8. Then you either refrigerate or serve right away

**Nutrition Information
Amount per serving 1 slice (28.0g)**
Calories: 46
Fat: 2.4g
Protein: 4.6g
Dietary Fiber: 0.4g
Carbohydrates: 1.1g

Spicy Spare Ribs Recipe

Ingredients
2 tablespoons of gochujang or hot pepper paste
1 tablespoon of raw honey
3 tablespoons of coconut aminos (it is a Paleo-friendly replacement for soy sauce)
Sea salt and freshly ground black pepper to taste
2 lbs. of pork spare ribs
2 garlic cloves (minced)
1 medium onion (sliced)
2 tablespoons of rice wine vinegar (this is Paleo; because there is no actual rice in it)
A thumb of fresh ginger (minced)

Directions:
1. First, you combine the gochujang, vinegar, garlic, honey, onion, coconut aminos, and ginger in a bowl.

2. After which you give everything a good stir and season to taste with salt and pepper.

3. After that, you rub the marinade all over the ribs and refrigerate overnight.

4. Meanwhile, you heat your oven to a temperature of 350 F.

5. At this point, you remove the ribs from the marinade and set the marinade aside.

6. Then you place the ribs in a roasting pan and cover with foil.

7. Furthermore, you roast in the oven for about 40 to 45 minutes.

8. After which you remove the foil covering the ribs and baste with the remaining marinade.

9. Finally, you cook the ribs for another 45 minutes, basting every 15 minutes.

Nutrition Information
Amount per serving 1(374)
Calories: 1085.5
Fat: 81g
Protein: 67.1g
Dietary Fiber: 0.1g
Carbohydrates: 17.2g

Pork and Apple Meatloaf Recipe

Ingredients
3 cups of apples (peeled and grated)
2 tablespoons of chili powder
2 teaspoons of dry mustard
Sea salt and freshly ground black pepper to taste
3 lb. of ground pork
2 small onions (minced)
2 teaspoons of ground cinnamon
14 slices of bacon (or more if desire)
Applesauce

Directions:
1. Meanwhile, you heat your oven to a temperature of 350 F.

2. Then you line a baking sheet with parchment.

3. After that, you combine the meat, apples, onion, chili powder, cinnamon, in a bowl and season with salt and pepper to taste.

4. At this point, you shape the meat mixture into a loaf on the baking sheet.

5. After which you arrange the bacon across the top, and tighten underneath the meatloaf.

6. Then you place the loaf in the oven and bake for about an hour.

7. Finally, you set the oven to broil and broil for about 3 to 5 minutes or until the bacon is crispy.

8. When serving, you serve the meatloaf with the applesauce.

Nutrition Information
Amount per serving 1(360)
Calories: 600.9
Fat: 37.1g
Protein: 39.1g
Dietary Fiber: 2.7g
Carbohydrates: 26.3g

Chicken with Mushroom Cream Sauce

Ingredients
2 medium shallots (minced)
4 tablespoons of fresh chives (minced)
8 tablespoons of full-fat coconut milk
Sea salt and freshly ground black pepper to taste
8 boneless, skinless chicken breasts
2 cups of mushrooms (thinly sliced)
1 cup of chicken stock
2 tablespoons of extra-virgin olive oil

Directions:
1. Meanwhile, you heat your oven to a temperature of 350 F.

2. After which you place the chicken breast in a casserole dish and bake for about 30 to 40 minutes.

3. At a point when the chicken is almost done, you heat the oil in a skillet over a medium heat.

4. After that, you add the shallots to the skillet and cook for about 30 seconds, then add the mushrooms and cook for about 2 to 3 minutes until tender.

5. Then you pour in the broth and cook for around 2 minutes.

6. After which you stir in the coconut milk and chives.

7. Finally, you bring to a simmer and cook for a minute and once the chicken is done, you cover it with the mushroom sauce and serve.

Nutrition Information
Amount per serving ()
Calories: 290

Fat: 7.0g
Protein: 21.0g
Dietary Fiber: 2.0g

Chicken and Artichoke Panzanella Recipe

Ingredients
2 cups of artichoke hearts, frozen or fresh
¾ cup of fresh basil (chopped)
2 cups of skinless, boneless chicken breast (diced, cooked)
3 large tomatoes (cut into small wedges)
1 cup of black olives (halved)
Ingredient for the Panzanella Vinaigrette
2 tablespoons of white wine vinegar
Sea salt and freshly ground black pepper to taste
2/3-cup of extra-virgin olive oil
1 tablespoon of freshly pressed lemon juice

Directions:
1. First, you heat a grill to medium-high.

2. After which you drizzle some olive oil on the artichoke hearts and season to taste.

3. After that, you grill the artichoke for about 2 minutes on each side, or until golden-brown.

4. At this point, you transfer them to a large salad bowl.

5. Then you add the chicken, the tomatoes, the olives, and the fresh basil to the bowl, and toss to combine.

6. This is the when you combine the ingredients in a small bowl, for the vinaigrette.

7. After which you season to taste and mix thoroughly.

8. Finally, you drizzle the vinaigrette over the salad, toss, and serve.

**Nutrition Information
Amount per serving ()**
Calories: 261
Fat: 13g
Protein: 42g
Dietary Fiber: 4g

Grilled Chicken and Pineapple with Onion Relish Recipe

Ingredients
3 fresh jalapeño peppers (thinly sliced)
6 boneless, skinless chicken breasts
6 pineapple (slices)
Ingredients for the onion relish
3 tablespoons of honey (it is optional)
4 ½ tablespoons of red wine
Sea salt and freshly ground black pepper to taste
6 to 9 red or yellow onions (thinly sliced)
4 ½ tablespoons of balsamic vinegar
3 tablespoons of olive oil

Directions:
1. Meanwhile, you heat a grill or BBQ to medium-high.

2. After which you warm the olive oil and sauté the onions in a skillet placed over a medium heat for about 10 min until caramelized.

3. After that, you add the honey, if using, and stir until dissolved; then you add the vinegar and the wine.

4. At this point, you simmer for about 10 minutes until all the liquid has evaporated, and season to taste.

5. Then you grill the chicken breast on the preheated BBQ until done (it will take you about 5 minutes per side).

6. This is when you place the pineapple slices and the jalapeño slices on the grill and grill them for about 2 min.

7. Finally, you top each chicken breast with jalapeño, pineapple, and onion relish, and serve.

Nutrition Information
Amount per serving 1(572)
Calories: 599.5
Fat: 33.5g
Protein: 47.2g
Dietary Fiber: 2.1g
Carbohydrates: 25.7g

Sun-dried Tomato Chicken Recipe

Ingredients
4 green onions (thinly sliced)
½ cup of sun-dried tomatoes (chopped)
2 teaspoons of dried oregano
Sea salt and freshly ground black pepper to taste
8 lbs. of chicken drumsticks (with or without the skin)
½ cup of olive oil
4 tablespoons of balsamic vinegar
2-garlic cloves (minced)

Directions:
1. Meanwhile, you heat your oven to a temperature of 350 F.

2. After which you combine the sun-dried tomatoes, balsamic vinegar, oregano, garlic, olive oil in a bowl, and season with salt and pepper to taste.

3. After that, you arrange the drumsticks in a single layer in a cooking dish, and pour the tomato mixture on top.

4. Then you sprinkle the green onions over everything in the dish, and bake for about 45 minutes, or until the chicken is well cooked.

Nutrition Information
Amount per serving ()
Calories: 320
Fat: 3.0g
Protein: 8g

Thai Larb Recipe

Ingredients
½ cup of green onions (coarsely chopped)
2 lime leaves (thinly sliced)
2 garlic cloves (thinly sliced)
3 tablespoons of extra-virgin olive oil
A fresh cilantro leaves
½ teaspoon of Sriracha sauce (it is optional)
1 ½ lb. of boneless skinless chicken breasts (cut into 1-inch pieces)
2 tablespoons of lemongrass (thinly sliced)
1 small red chili (thinly sliced)
2 tablespoons and 1 tablespoon of fish sauce
Boston (or romaine lettuce leaves)
1 lime (quartered)
1/3 cup of fresh lime juice

Directions:
1. First, you combine the chicken, green onions, lemongrass, lime leaves, red chili, and garlic, 2 teaspoons of the fish sauce, salt and pepper to taste, and 1 tbsp. of olive oil in a food processor.

2. After which you pulse until the chicken is finely chopped.

3. After that, you combine the lime juice, the remaining 1-tablespoon of fish sauce, and the Sriracha sauce in a small bowl.

4. At this point, you warm the remaining olive oil in a large skillet, over medium-high heat.

5. Then you add the chicken mixture and sauté until chicken turns golden-brown, about 6 to 8 minutes.

6. Finally, you top the lettuce leaves with the chicken mixture, garnish with cilantro leaves, and drizzle some lime sauce on top.

7. After which you serve with some lime.

Nutrition Information
Amount per serving (153.7g)
Calories: 238
Fat: 8.8g
Protein: 34g
Dietary Fiber: 0.7g
Carbohydrates: 4.4g

Zaatar Grilled Chicken Recipe

Ingredients
½ cup of olive oil
4 tablespoons of lemon juice
Sea salt and freshly ground black pepper to taste
8 chicken thighs
4 tablespoons of zaatar (check ingredients below)
2 teaspoons of lemon zest
2 garlic cloves (minced)

Ingredients for the Zaatar
4 tablespoons of dried thyme
4 tablespoons of dried oregano
½ cup of sumac
2 tablespoons of dried basil
4 tablespoons of dried marjoram

Directions:
1. Meanwhile, you heat a grill or BBQ to medium high.

2. After which you combine the entire ingredients for the zaatar in a small bowl, and mix well.

3. After that, you whisk together the olive oil, the zaatar, the lemon juice, the lemon zest, the garlic, in another bowl, and season with salt and pepper to taste.

4. At this point, you dip each piece of chicken in the mixture, making sure they are all well coated.

5. Finally, you place the chicken on the grill and cook on each side until well done, about 7 to 8 minutes per side.

6. Make sure you serve hot.

**Nutrition Information
Amount per serving ()**
Calories: 406
Protein: 27g
Dietary Fiber: 1.49g
Carbohydrates: 4.8g

Spicy drumstick recipe

Ingredients
6 cloves garlic (minced)
2 teaspoons of garlic powder
20 chicken drumsticks
6 tablespoons of coconut oil (clarified butter or another paleo fat, melted)
4 teaspoons of chili powder
Sea salt and freshly ground black pepper to taste

Directions:
1. Meanwhile, you heat your oven to a temperature of 375 F.

2. After which you combine the garlic, chili powder, garlic powder, salt and pepper in a large bowl, as well as the cooking fat.

3. At this point, you dump in the chicken and mix well to ensure all the meat coats evenly with the seasonings.

4. After that, you place the chicken drumsticks on a large baking sheet with space in between each to prevent overlap.

5. Then you cook for about an hour, until the chicken is well cooked, turning the pieces once during the cooking process.

Nutrition Information
Amount per serving 1(250g)
Calories: 393.2
Fat: 16.2g
Protein: 35.4g
Dietary Fiber: 0.7g
Carbohydrates: 23.5g

Grilled Pork with Basil Rub Recipe

Ingredients
4 garlic cloves (minced)
4 tablespoons of fresh lemon juice
Sea salt and freshly ground black pepper to taste
8 bone-in pork loin chops
2 cups of fresh basil leave (minced)
4 tablespoons of extra-virgin olive oil

Directions:
1. First, you combine the garlic, basil, lemon juice, olive oil, in a bowl, and season with salt and pepper to taste.

2. After which you spread the rub on both side of the pork chops, and marinate for about 30 to 45 minutes.

3. Meanwhile, you heat your grill to a medium high heat.

4. Then you place the chops on the grill, and cook for approximately 6 minutes per side, or until the chops are just cooked through.

Nutrition Information
Amount per serving 1(289)
Calories: 66.7
Fat: 6.8g
Protein: 0.4g
Dietary Fiber: 0.3g
Carbohydrates: 1.4g

Spicy Pork Chili Recipe

Ingredients
2 onions (finely sliced)
2 bell of peppers (sliced)
28 oz. can of tomatoes, diced
2 tablespoons of smoked paprika
¼ teaspoon of ground cayenne pepper
3 tablespoons of red wine vinegar
Sea salt and freshly ground black pepper to taste
4 ¼ lbs. of boneless pork shoulder (fat removed)
2 red chilies (seeded and finely chopped)
4 garlic cloves (minced)
¼ cup of chili powder
1 tablespoon of ground cumin
Small bunch fresh oregano leaves (minced)
¼ cup of extra-virgin olive oil

Directions:
1. Meanwhile, you heat your oven to a temperature of 350 F.

2. After which you warm the olive oil in an ovenproof stew pot over a medium heat.

3. After that, you add the garlic, onions, and red chilies, and cook for about 3 to 5 minutes or until the onions are soft.

4. At this point, you lower the heat and add the bell peppers, diced tomatoes, chili powder, smoked paprika, cumin, cayenne pepper, oregano leaves, and salt and pepper to taste.

5. Then you place the pork shoulder in the pot, give everything a little shake, then add the red wine vinegar, and pour in enough water to just cover the meat.

6. Finally, you bring to a boil, cover, and place in the oven for about 3 hours.

Note that the chili is done when you can easily break the meat apart with a fork.

Nutrition Information
Amount per serving ()
Calories: 315.0
Fat: 22.6g
Protein: 12.8g
Dietary Fiber: 2.4g
Carbohydrates: 15.6g

Pork Tenderloin with Burgundy Sauce Recipe

Ingredients
4 red onions (thinly sliced)
8 garlic cloves (minced)
2 cups of water
Sea salt and freshly ground black pepper to taste
4 lbs. of pork tenderloin
2-stalk celery (chopped)
2 cups of red wine
4 tablespoons of tapioca starch

Directions:
1. First, you heat your oven to a temperature of 350 F.

2. After which you season the pork tenderloin with sea salt and black pepper on both sides.

3. After that, you place the pork in a baking dish and sprinkle garlic over the pork, top with the onion and celery, and pour the wine and water over everything.

4. Bake for approximately 45 to 50 minutes in the oven.

5. At a point when the cooking is done, you remove the pork from the dish and add everything else from the baking dish into a saucepan over a medium heat.

6. Then you bring the sauce to a boil and slowly whisk in the tapioca starch until it thickens, and season to taste with salt and pepper.

7. Finally, you slice the tenderloin, pour the sauce over it, and serve.

**Nutrition Information
Amount per serving 1(494g)**
Calories: 902.5
Fat: 61.9g
Protein: 48.4g
Carbohydrates: 6.5g

Crab Stuffed Shrimp Recipe

Ingredients
2 (6oz.) can of lump crabmeat (preferably, well-drained)
½ teaspoons of poultry seasoning
Old Bay seasoning (it is optional)
2 lbs. of cooked wild shrimp (preferable the large ones)
5 tablespoons of Paleo mayonnaise
¼ teaspoon of black pepper

Tips:
1. If the shrimp is frozen, I suggest you thaw according to the package.

2. Remember that the crab mixture should be on the dryer side, not overly wet from the mayonnaise.

Directions:
1. First, you slice the back of the shrimp starting from the top all the way to the tail.

2. After that, you make sure not to go all the way through but deep enough to hold the crabmeat.

3. After which you combine the well-drained crabmeat, mayonnaise, poultry seasoning, and black pepper in a small bowl.

4. At this point, you stuff each shrimp with the crab.

5. Then you sprinkle with Old Bay Seasoning if you wish.

6. Make sure you serve with lemon wedges and cocktail sauce.

Nutrition Information
Amount per serving 1(1158)

Calories: 87.8
Fat: 6.1g
Protein: 3.3g
Dietary Fiber: 0.2g
Carbohydrates: 3.3g

Smoked Salmon Salad in Cucumber Slices

Ingredients
½ cup of green onions (finely chopped)
4 tablespoons of drained capers (it is optional)
Sea salt and freshly ground black pepper to taste
2 (12 oz.) smoked salmon (coarsely chopped)
6 tablespoons of homemade mayonnaise
2 tablespoons of fresh dill (chopped + some for garnishing)
2-4 English cucumbers (sliced)

Directions:
1. First, you combine the green onions, dill, capers, and mayonnaise in a bowl.

2. After which you add the chopped salmon, give the mixture a good stir, and season to taste.

3. After that, you make each cucumber slice into a small cup by scooping out the center with a small spoon, leaving the bottom intact.

4. Then you fill each cucumber cup with the salmon mixture.

5. Finally, you sprinkle some fresh dill, season to taste, and then serve.

Nutrition Information
Amount per serving 1(29g)
Calories: 20
Fat: 1.4g
Protein: 0.9g
Dietary Fiber: 0.4g
Carbohydrates: 1.2g

Pomegranate Salmon Recipe

Ingredients
Juice of 2 lemons
2 teaspoons of sumac
Seeds from 2 pomegranates
Sea salt and freshly ground black pepper to taste
8 wild-caught salmon fillets
2 tablespoons of fresh thyme (minced)
4 teaspoons of pomegranate molasses
Cooking fat

Directions:
1. First, you drizzle on the salmon fillets with the lemon juice and sprinkle the thyme on top.

2. After which you season to taste with salt and pepper and refrigerate for about 30 minutes.

3. After that, you place a skillet over a medium heat and add in some cooking fat.

4. Then you add the salmon to the hot skillet and cook for about 6 to 8 minutes.

5. At this point, you pour the sumac and pomegranate molasses over the fillet.

6. Finally, you turn over and cook for another 5 to 6 minutes.

7. Make sure you serve with pomegranate seeds sprinkled on top.

Nutrition Information
Amount per serving 1(478g)
Calories: 617.3
Fat: 26.0g
Protein: 68.0g
Dietary Fiber: 5.2g
Carbohydrates: 27.1g

Grilled Maple Dijon Salmon with Bacon

Ingredients
4 slices bacon (cooked and crumbled)
6 cloves garlic (minced)
Sea salt and freshly ground black pepper to taste
A 3 lbs. fresh salmon filet (skin-on)
6 tablespoons of Dijon (or homemade mustard)
3 tablespoons of maple syrup or raw honey;

Directions:
1. Meanwhile, you heat your grill or BBQ to a medium-high heat.

2. After which you combine the maple syrup, Dijon mustard, and garlic in a bowl.

3. After that, you season the salmon to taste with sea salt and freshly ground black pepper.

4. At this point, you spread the entire Maple-Dijon mixture on top of the salmon.

5. Then you place the salmon on the grill, skin side down first and cook for about 6 minutes per side.

6. Finally, you remove the salmon from the grill, sprinkle some crumbled bacon on top, and serve.

Nutrition Information
Amount per serving 1(219g)
Calories: 273.5
Fat: 10.9g
Protein: 34.3g
Dietary Fiber: 0.1g
Carbohydrates: 8.1g

Lomi Lomi Salmon

Ingredients
4 plum tomatoes (seeded and diced)
½ cup of fresh cilantro (chopped)
4 tablespoons of extra virgin olive oil
2 tablespoons of coconut oil
2 lbs. of wild salmon, skinless (cut into small cubes)
8 scallions (thinly sliced)
2 jalapeño pepper, seeded and minced (it is optional)
Juice of 2 lime

Directions:
1. First, you warm up the coconut oil and add the cubed salmon on a skillet placed over a medium high heat.

2. After which you season to taste with sea salt and black pepper.

3. After that, you cook for about 2 to 3 minutes, until just cooked, and then let cool down.

4. At this point, you combine the tomatoes, the scallions, the cilantro, the jalapeño, the cooked salmon, the lime juice and the olive oil in a bowl.

5. Then you toss gently to coat everything, and serve cold.

Nutrition Information
Amount per serving 1(cup)
Calories: 150
Fat: 5.2g
Protein: 17.7g
Dietary Fiber: 2.11g

Tuna with Avocado Salsa

Ingredients
Sea salt and freshly ground black pepper to taste
4 (6 oz.) pieces of fresh of tuna
½ teaspoon of ground coriander
Ingredients for the Avocado Salsa
1 jalapeno pepper (minced, it is optional)
2 avocados (peeled and diced)
2 tablespoons of lime juice (freshly squeezed)
3 plum tomatoes (seeded and diced)
Sea salt and freshly ground pepper to taste
1 red onion (minced)
2 tablespoons of fresh cilantro (minced)

Directions:
1. First, you combine the entire ingredients for the salsa in a medium bowl.

2. After which you season to taste with sea salt and freshly ground black pepper, and combine well.

3. After that, you refrigerate the salsa for about 2 to 4 hours to bring out the flavors.

4. Meanwhile, you heat your grill to a medium high heat.

5. At this point, you sprinkle coriander over the tuna steaks and season to taste with sea salt and black pepper.

6. Then you grill the tuna for about 2 to 3 minutes per side.

7. Finally, you serve the grilled tuna with the avocado salsa on top.

Nutrition Information
Amount per serving 1(1/2 cup)
Calories: 138
Fat: 9g
Protein: 11g
Dietary Fiber: 4g
Carbohydrates: 5g

Scallop Tartare with Strawberries Recipe

Ingredients
4-6 strawberries (thinly chopped)
The juice from a whole lemon
Sea salt and freshly ground black pepper to taste
12 scallops (thinly diced)
2 tablespoons of green onions (minced)
2 tablespoons of olive oil
1 tablespoons of fresh basil (minced)

Directions:
1. First, you combine the scallops, the strawberries, the green onions and the basil in a bowl.

2. After which you pour in the lemon juice and the olive oil, give everything a good stir.

3. After that, you season to taste with sea salt and black pepper and stir again.

4. Then you serve cold.

Nutrition Information
Amount per serving (15)
Calories: 231.9
Fat: 9.4g
Protein: 34.2g
Dietary Fiber: 0.3g
Carbohydrates: 0.8g

Grilled Salmon-Tomato Skewers Recipe

Ingredients
48 cherry tomatoes
8 teaspoons of extra-virgin olive oil
6 garlic cloves (minced)
24 bamboo skewers
2 lbs. of salmon fillet cut in 1-inch cubes
6 teaspoons of fresh rosemary (minced)
4 teaspoons of lemon juice
2 Lemon (sliced)
Sea salt and freshly ground black pepper to taste

Directions:
1. Meanwhile, you heat your grill to a medium-high heat.

2. After which you combine the olive oil, rosemary, garlic, and lemon juice in a bowl.

3. After that, you add sea salt and freshly ground black pepper to taste, and whisk everything together.

4. Then you add the salmon and cherry tomatoes and marinate for about 30 minutes.

5. At this point, you load up each skewer, alternating tomatoes with pieces of salmon.

6. At a point when the grill is hot, you BBQ the skewers, until the salmon is well done.

7. Furthermore, you turn them carefully when the first side cooks, since fish can break easily.

8. You should expect the fish to be ready in about 6 to 10 minutes.

9. Finally, you serve with a fresh slice of lemon and garnish with rosemary.

Nutrition Information
Amount per serving ()
Calories: 172
Protein: 23g
Dietary Fiber: 1g
Carbohydrates: 4g

Oysters Kilpatrick Recipe

Ingredients
Two slices of Canadian bacon, back bacon (shredded)
1 tablespoons of fresh parsley (minced)
A Several handfuls of rock salt to stabilize the oysters (it is optional)
12 oysters (shucked)
Worcestershire sauce to taste, on each oyster (it is optional)
3-4 lemon wedges (to serve)
A Freshly ground black pepper to taste

Directions:
1. Meanwhile, you heat a grill on medium-high heat.

2. After which you place a thick layer of rock salt on a baking tray, and place the oysters on top (Note that this is optional if you do not have enough rock salt; it is just there to stabilize the oysters and ensure that you don't lose any juice or moisture)

3. After that, you sprinkle a drop or two of Worcestershire sauce over each oyster.

4. Then you add the bacon bits to the oysters, and place on the grill for at least 10 minutes. (If you want to save some time, I suggest you pre-cook the bacon)

5. At a point when the cooking is complete, you sprinkle with the fresh parsley and serve with lemon wedges.

Nutrition Information
Amount per serving 1(381g)
Calories: 490
Fat: 29.4g

Protein: 34.2g
Carbohydrates: 20.3g

Roasted asparagus

Ingredients
2 tablespoons of olive oil
½ teaspoons of garlic powder
1 teaspoons of fresh lemon juice
2 bunches asparagus
½ teaspoon of sea salt
A Freshly ground black pepper to taste;

Directions:
1. Meanwhile, you heat your oven to a temperature of 400 F.

2. After which you remove the tough part off the asparagus stalks.

3. After that, you spread the asparagus out on a large baking sheet.

4. Then you drizzle with olive oil and lemon juice.

5. At this point, you sprinkle with salt, pepper and garlic powder.

6. Finally, you toss the asparagus to ensure that all of it coat evenly and cook for about 10 minutes, flipping once after 5 minutes.

Nutrition Information
Amount per serving 1(60.4)
Calories: 41
Fat: 3.4g
Protein: 1.2g
Dietary Fiber: 1.2g
Carbohydrates: 2.2g

Cuban Shredded Beef Recipe

Ingredients
6 garlic cloves (minced)
1 teaspoons of ground cumin
1 teaspoon of lime zest
2 cups of beef stock
Lime wedges (for serving)
4 lbs. of boneless beef chuck
2 onions (thinly sliced)
4 tablespoons of fresh orange juice
2 tablespoons of lime juice
Cooking fat
Sea salt and freshly ground black pepper

Directions:
1. First, you season the beef all over with sea salt and black pepper to taste.

2. After which you place the beef in a slow cooker with the stock and cook for 6 to 8 hours on low.

3. After that, when the beef is cooked, break it apart gently with a fork and set aside.

4. At this point, you melt the cooking fat in a large skillet placed over a medium-high heat.

5. Then you add the garlic and onion, and cook for about 5 minutes until the onion is golden and soft.

6. Furthermore, you add the beef to the skillet.

7. After which you reduce the heat to medium and cook for about 4 minutes.

8. Then you add the cumin, orange juice, lime juice, lime zest, and season again with salt and pepper to taste.

9. Finally, you give everything a good stir and then serve warm with lime wedges.

Nutrition Information
Amount per serving 1(289g)
Calories: 715.3
Fat: 57.9g
Protein: 42.1g
Dietary Fiber: 0.4g
Carbohydrates: 4.9g

Barbecued Sirloin in Dijon Recipe

Ingredients
4 tablespoons of fresh basil (coarsely chopped)
2 tablespoons of Dijon mustard
4 tablespoons of white wine vinegar
4 lbs. of beef sirloin
4 tablespoons of ground black pepper
2 tablespoon of extra-virgin olive oil;

Directions:
1. First, you combine the basil, the black pepper, the olive oil, the Dijon mustard and the white wine vinegar in a bowl.

2. After which you rub the marinade onto the sirloin and refrigerate for about 1½ hours.

3. Meanwhile, you heat the BBQ or grill to medium-high, and cook the sirloin for about 12 to 15 minutes on each side.

4. Finally, you let the meat rest around 15 minutes before serving.

Nutrition Information
Amount per serving 1(272g)
Calories: 493.0
Fat: 34.7g
Protein: 31.9g
Dietary Fiber: 0.6g
Carbohydrates: 4.5g

Simple Summer Chicken Recipe

Ingredients
1 cup of lemon juice
4 teaspoons of Italian seasoning
Sea salt and freshly ground black pepper to taste
8 skinless, boneless chicken breasts
1 teaspoon of onion powder
4 garlic cloves (minced)

Directions:
1. Meanwhile, you heat your grill to a medium-high heat.

2. After which you place the chicken in a marinating container (preferably, glass or ceramic; not metal) and drizzle with the lemon juice, onion powder, Italian seasoning, garlic.

3. After that, you season each breast to taste.

4. At this point, you let the chicken marinate for about 20 minutes.

5. Then you cook on the prepared grill for about 10 to 15 minutes per side, or until cooked through.

6. Make sure you serve warm with extra lemon wedges.

Nutrition Information
Amount per serving 1(558)
Calories: 415.7
Fat: 15.4g
Protein: 36.0g
Dietary Fiber: 8.0g

Grilled Chicken with Lime Butter Recipe

Ingredients
2 tablespoons of chili powder
2 tablespoons of honey (it is optional)
6 tablespoons of olive oil
Sea salt and freshly ground black pepper to taste
7 to 8lb. bone-in chicken parts
2 tablespoons of ground cinnamon
2 teaspoons of unsweetened cocoa powder
2 tablespoons of balsamic vinegar
Ingredients for lime butter
1 cup of ghee (melted)
4 tablespoons of shallots (minced)
Freshly ground black pepper to taste
½ cup of chopped fresh cilantro
2 Serrano Chile, minced
2 tablespoons of fresh lime juice;

Directions:
1. Meanwhile, you heat your grill to a medium-high heat.

2. After which you combine the chili powder, ground cinnamon, cocoa powder, olive oil, balsamic vinegar, honey, if using, in a bowl and season with salt and pepper to taste.

3. After that, you mix until well blended.

4. At this point, you brush the chicken pieces with the sauce.

5. Then you place the chicken on grill and cook for about 30 min (or preferably, until the chicken is cooked; the exact time varies depending on what chicken parts you are using).

6. This is when you combine all the ingredients for the lime butter in a bowl.

7. After which you drizzle the lime butter over the chicken before serving.

Nutrition Information
Amount per serving 1(206g)
Calories: 580.7
Fat: 40.6g
Protein: 48.2g
Dietary Fiber: 0.9g
Carbohydrates: 3.7g

Kansas City BBQ Wings Recipe

Ingredients
Twenty chicken wings
Ingredients for the Kansas City BBQ sauce
3 garlic cloves (minced)
¼ cup of honey, it is optional
1½ tablespoons of chili powder
½ teaspoons of onion powder
Sea salt and freshly ground black pepper to taste
3 cups of homemade ketchup
¼ cup of apple cider vinegar
2 tablespoons of homemade Worcestershire sauce
1 teaspoon of smoked paprika
1 teaspoon of cayenne pepper

Directions:
1. Meanwhile, you heat your oven to a temperature of 425 F.

2. After which you combine all the ingredients for the Kansas City BBQ sauce in a bowl and season to taste with salt and pepper.

3. After that, you combine the chicken wings with the BBQ sauce, in a large bowl, and toss gently to coat.

4. Then you place the chicken wings on a baking sheet and line them up in a single layer.

5. Finally, you bake in the oven for approximately 20 to 25 minutes.

6. Make sure you serve warm.

Nutrition Information
Amount per serving (10.4 oz.)
Calories: 520
Fat: 25g
Protein: 75g
Dietary Fiber: 1g
Carbohydrates: 1g

BBQ Chicken and Bacon Bites Recipe

Ingredients
2 lbs. bacon (preferable, store-bought or make your own), with each slice cut in half
Toothpicks
8 boneless, skinless chicken breasts (cut into cubes)
1 cup of homemade BBQ sauce

Directions:
1. Meanwhile, you heat your oven to a temperature of 350 F.

2. After which you wrap each chicken piece with a half-slice of bacon and secure with a toothpick.

3. After that, you brush each chicken bite with BBQ sauce.

4. Then you place in the oven and bake for about 15 to 20 minutes.

5. At this point, you turn the chicken bites over, and brush again with BBQ sauce.

6. Finally, you place back in the oven for another 15 to 20 minutes.

7. Make sure you serve warm.

Nutrition Information
Amount per serving 1(163g)
Calories: 36.7
Fat: 3.6g
Protein: 0.7g
Carbohydrates: 0.3g

Chicken with Lime and Avocado Salad Recipe

Ingredients for the chicken
2 onions (sliced thinly)
4 teaspoons of ground coriander
½ cup of tomato pasta
Lime wedges (to serve)
12 chicken thigh fillets (cut into pieces)
4 teaspoons of ground cumin
4 teaspoons of smoked paprika
Cooking fat

Ingredients for the salad
4 ripe tomatoes (seeded and chopped)
2 tablespoons of jalapeño chili (minced)
½ cup of fresh cilantro
2 head romaine lettuce (torn into bite-size pieces)
2 ripe avocados (cut into cubes)
1 red onion (chopped)
2 tablespoons of lime juice
½ cup of extra-virgin olive oil

Directions:
1. First, you add some cooking fat to a large skillet that placed over a medium-high heat.

2. After which you add the chicken and cook, stirring frequently, until the meat is browned and cooked through.

3. After that, you add the onions, pasta, cumin, coriander, and paprika.

4. At this point, you keep stirring while you cook everything for another 2-3 minutes or until the onions are soft and tender.

5. Combine the entire ingredients for the salad in a large bowl, and give everything a good stir.

6. Then you divide the cooked chicken among plates and top with the salad.

7. Make sure you serve with some lime wedges.

Nutrition Information
Amount per serving 1(127g)
Calories: 194.6
Fat: 17.2g
Protein: 2.2g
Dietary Fiber: 7.0g
Carbohydrates: 11.7g

Turkey Chili Recipe

Ingredients
4 cups of carrots (sliced or diced)
4 bell pepper (chopped)
4 tablespoons of tomato paste
2 cups of chicken (or turkey stock)
2 tablespoons of ground cumin
2 teaspoons of dried oregano
Green onions, sliced (it is optional, for garnishing)
6 to 8 cups of shredded, cooked turkey meat
4 cups of onions (chopped)
4 cups of diced tomatoes
8 garlic cloves (minced)
4 tablespoons of chili powder or to taste
2 tablespoons of dried hot red pepper flakes
Paleo cooking fat
Sea salt and freshly ground black pepper to taste

Directions:
1. First, you melt some cooking fat in a large saucepan placed over a medium-high heat, and cook the onions, bell peppers and carrots for about 5 minutes until the onions are golden.

2. After which you add the garlic, chili powder, cumin, red pepper flakes, and oregano.

3. After that, you stir well and cook for a minute.

4. Then you add the tomato paste, diced tomatoes, chicken or turkey stock, cooked turkey meat, and season with salt and pepper to taste.

5. At this point, you give everything a good stir and then bring the chili to a simmer, reducing the heat to low, and let it simmer, uncovered, for about 30 to 45 minutes.

6. Make sure you serve warm with freshly sliced green onions on top.

Nutrition Information
Amount per serving 1(336g)
Calories: 310.6
Fat: 13.7g
Protein: 23.1g
Dietary Fiber: 8.5g

Slow Cooked Bacon-Wrapped Chicken Recipe

Ingredients
3 cups of homemade BBQ sauce
8 apples (peeled and chopped)
16 to 24 slices bacon
8 boneless skinless chicken breasts
4 tablespoons of fresh lemon juice
2 onions (diced)

Directions:
1. First, you wrap each chicken breast with bacon slices.

2. After which you place each bacon-wrapped chicken breast in your slow cooker.

3. After that, you combine the BBQ sauce, lemon juice, apples, and onions in a bowl, and mix thoroughly.

4. At this point, you pour the BBQ sauce mixture over the chicken.

5. Then you cover and cook on low for about 6 to 8 hours.

6. Finally, you serve the chicken breasts topped with the apple and onion mixture.

Nutrition Information
Amount per serving 1(260g)
Calories: 419.0
Fat: 27.1g
Protein: 33.3g
Dietary Fiber: 0.1g
Carbohydrates: 8.8g

Spicy Sriracha Chicken Wings Recipe

Ingredients
2 teaspoons of garlic powder
2 tablespoons of fresh cilantro leave, minced
4 lbs. of chicken wings
Sea salt and freshly ground black pepper, to taste
Ingredients for the Sriracha-based sauce
½ cup of raw honey (it is optional)
Juice of two limes
10 tablespoons of olive oil
½ cup of sriracha sauce
2 tablespoons of coconut aminos;

Directions:
1. Meanwhile, you heat your oven to a temperature of 400 F.

2. After which you combine the olive oil, honey, sriracha, coconut aminos, and lime juice in a small bowl.

3. After that, you combine the chicken wings, garlic powder, in a large bowl, and season with salt and pepper to taste.

4. At this point, you arrange the wings on a parchment paper covered baking sheet and bake for about 25-30 minutes, flipping them over halfway through.

5. Then you brush the wings with the Sriracha mixture and place them under the broiler for about 3-4 minutes, or until crisp and crusted.

6. Finally, you garnished with fresh cilantro and serve immediately.

Nutrition Information
Amount per serving 1(515)
Calories: 1720.1
Fat: 131.2g
Protein: 120g
Dietary Fiber: 2.0g
Carbohydrates: 7.8g

Honey-mustard Drumsticks Recipe

Ingredients
½ cup of Dijon (or homemade mustard)
6 cloves garlic (minced)
4 tablespoons of coconut aminos (it is optional)
Sea salt and freshly ground black pepper to taste
8 lbs. of chicken drumsticks (washed and patted dry)
4 tablespoons of mustard powder
2/3 cup of raw honey (it is optional)
Chives for garnishing

Directions:
1. First, you whisk together the Dijon mustard, mustard powder, honey, garlic, coconut aminos, and salt, and pepper to taste in a small bowl.

2. After which you pour the mustard marinade over the drumsticks and refrigerate them for at least 2 hours.

3. Meanwhile, you heat your grill to a medium-high.

4. At this point, you grill the drumsticks for about 25 to 30 minutes, turning every 5 minutes and basting with any leftover marinade.

5. Finally, when the chicken is cooked, you then sprinkle with fresh chives and serve

Nutrition Information
Amount per serving 1(186g)
Calories: 301
Fat: 13.0g
Protein: 29.7g
Dietary Fiber: 0.5g
Carbohydrates: 15g

Conclusion

To lose weight is very easy if you know the process and how to go about it. That is the reason for this Book, to help you achieve your weight loss goal in No time. Get in shape while eating the foods you love. Take advantage of this top new healthy and delicious recipes provided for you in this book.

Remember, the only bad action you can take is no action at all.

www.ingramcontent.com/pod-product-compliance
Lightning Source LLC
Chambersburg PA
CBHW081725100526
44591CB00016B/2502